Alan,

Let's Explore!

[signature]

I love you, Biska!
December 2022

EXPLORING AMERICA
A Photographic Journey

Photography by David Hares II

Rabbit Press

Copyright © 2015 by Rabbit Press
Photographs copyright © 2015 David Hares II

First Edition

All rights reserved. No part of this book may be reproduced or utilized in any form or by any means, electronic or mechanical, including photocopying, recording, or by any information storage or retrieval system, without permission in writing from the publisher.

Library of Congress Cataloging-in-Publication Data on file

ISBN: 978-1-944459-24-6

For the latest photographs, product, and additional information, visit HaresPhotography.com.

For information about special discounts for bulk purchases,
please contact Rabbit Press Special Sales: *RabbitPressPublishing@gmail.com*

Rabbit Press
P. O. Box 471624
Fort Worth, Texas 76147
Email: *RabbitPressPublishing@gmail.com*
Website: *RabbitPress.org*

Printed in United States

This book is a journey to explore our great country's National Parks and the places in between. So far my adventures have taken me over 40,000 miles in an attempt to capture the beauty and uniqueness of our country's treasures. These photographs are meant to trigger memories of times you may have spent in these wonderful places, to inspire you to see them again or experience them for the first time. Join me on this journey *Exploring America*.

Growing up I was fortunate because my dad had time off in the summer allowing us to travel and camp our way across the United States. My family (all 7 of us) would load up the van and our tent camper ready to take off for 6 weeks. We really couldn't afford a camera for me at that time, so I collected postcards from all the places we explored.

Upon graduating from college, I wanted one more adventure before heading off to the corporate world. With camera and job offer in hand, I explored the Western United States and Canada for 6 weeks. The trip covered 8400 miles, 12 states, 2 provinces in Canada, and 14 National Parks. While in the corporate world my travel adventures continued, but this travel was a lot different because it was only for 1 to 2 weeks at a time - most of it by plane. Being a road warrior, I got to know my travel agent so well that she became my wife. Between the travel agency and over 1 million AAdvantage miles we continued to explore the world.

In 2007 our lives suddenly changed; I lost my wife to a stroke. Unexpectedly, my two teenage children and I had to survive as a family. The answer was travel. We took many, many trips together and were able to remain strong as a family. My perspective on life changed drastically; I started to prepare for a life-long dream outside the corporate world... to explore and photograph the National Parks.

While I have always taken pictures, my desire was to become better at the craft. Thankfully, I met Peter Poulides of Dallas Center for Photography in Dallas and started to learn from this lifelong, professional photographer. Peter taught me to "Look where people don't look, see what people don't see..." Peter took my photography to the next level.

Rejuvenated, I bought a truck camper and was ready to travel, explore and photograph. My plan was to take a three month sabbatical as soon as my youngest left for college. Just before my daughter graduated, my company was going through layoffs. The path to recreate my post-college trip was clear - I volunteered and established HaresPhotography.com.

The first trip from May through November of 2012 covered many of the places from my college trip and added a few more including over 13,000 miles, 12 states, 2 provinces, and 19 National Parks. The exploration has continued and over the past few of years I have been able to share portions of my trips with both my son and daughter for weeks at a time. Through my travels, I was fortunate enough to meet a wonderful woman that has now joined me as my wife. The adventure continues...

For your enjoyment, there are many more pictures on my website: HaresPhotography.com.

Thank you for coming along on this travel journey with me.

David Hares II

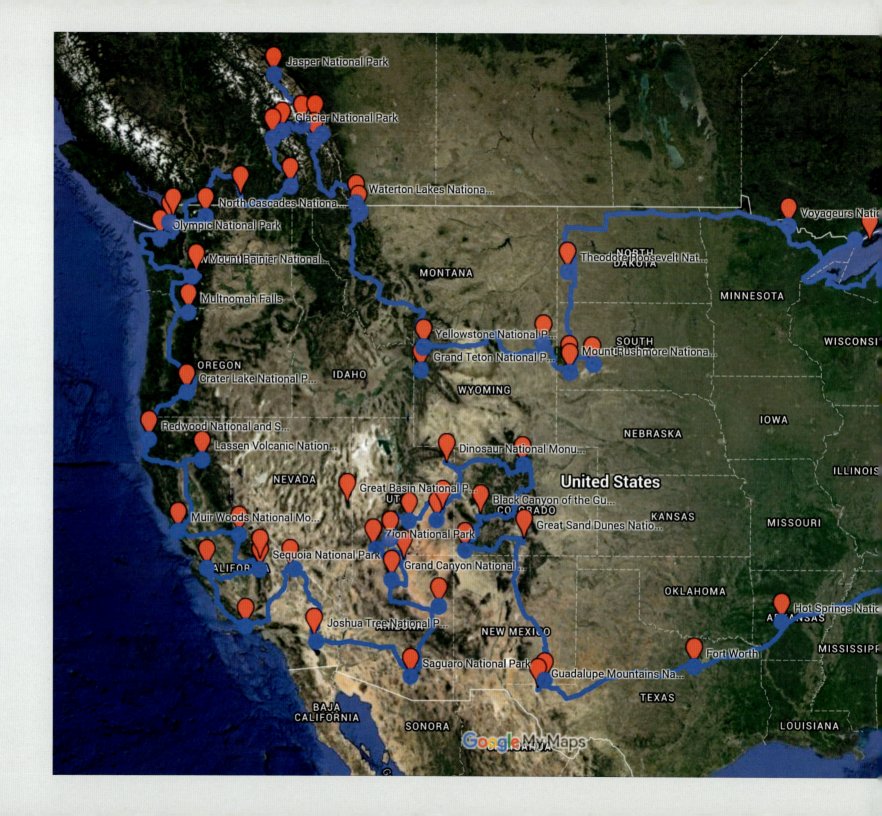

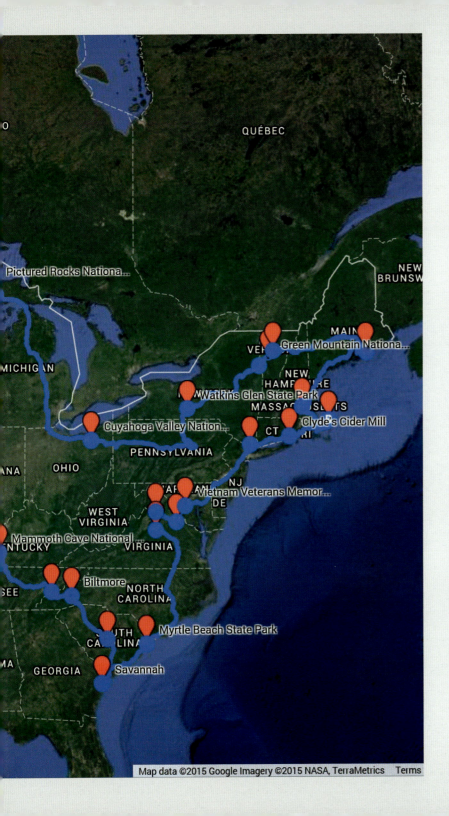

This map is a combination
of the trips from
May 2012 through October 2015.

It includes the details of the
routes and points of interest we
visited along the way.

A link to the map is available on page 96.

"Look where people don't look.
See what people don't see.
That's what makes an
interesting photograph."

Spruce Tree House
Mesa Verde
National Park,
Colorado

Cliff Palace
Mesa Verde National Park, Colorado

Hiking the Dunes
Great Sand Dunes National Park, Colorado

Painted Wall
Black Canyon of the Gunnison National Park, Colorado

Trout Lake Trestle
Uncompahgre National Forest, Colorado

Dead Horse Point Rainbow
Canyonlands National Park, Utah

Green River
Canyonlands National Park, Utah

Delicate Arch
Arches National Park, Utah

Landscape Arch
Arches National Park, Utah

Dino Bone Jam
Dinosaur National Monument, Utah

Bryce Point
Bryce Canyon National Park, Utah

Super Moon Eclipse
Bryce Canyon National Park, Utah

Bryce by Super Moonlight
Bryce Canyon National Park, Utah

Observation Point
Zion National Park, Utah

The Narrows
Zion
National Park,
Utah

Bright Angel Point View
North Rim - Grand Canyon National Park, Arizona

Horseshoe Bend
Glen Canyon National Recreation Area, Arizona

Walhalla Overlook
North Rim - Grand Canyon National Park, Arizona

Powell Point
South Rim - Grand Canyon National Park, Arizona

Crystal Forest
Petrified Forest National Park, Arizona

Under the Rainbow
Petrified Forest National Park, Arizona

Painted Desert
Petrified Forest National Park, Arizona

Saguaro Sunrise
Saguaro National Park, Arizona

Joshua Tree
Joshua Tree National Park, California

Patient Coyote
Death Valley National Park, California

Ancient Sequoia
Sequoia National Park, California

Giant Forest
Sequoia National Park, California

Tunnel View
Yosemite National Park, California

Tunnel View by Full Moonlight
Yosemite National Park, California

Half Dome
Yosemite National Park, California

Vernal Fall
Yosemite National Park, California

Avenue of the Giants
Redwood National Park, California

Foggy Morning
Redwood National Park, California

Wizard Island

Crater Lake National Park, Oregon

Old Tree
Crater Lake National Park, Oregon

Multnomah Falls
Columbia River Gorge National Scenic Area, Oregon

Lower Falls
Columbia River Gorge
National Scenic Area,
Oregon

Sol Duc Falls
Olympic National Park, Washington

Ancient Northwest
Moran State Park, Washington

Previous Page:
Hurricane Ridge
Olympic National Park, Washington

Dad Greeting the Mountain
Mount Rainier National Park, Washington

Sunning Fox
San Juan Islands National Monument, Washington

Intense Eagle
San Juan Island National Historic Park, Washington

Eagle Trio
San Juan Island National Historic Park, Washington

Sunbeam Kayak
San Juan Islands National Monument, Washington

Lighthouse Sunset
San Juan Island
(Places In Between),
Washington

Fourth of July Reflections
San Juan Islands National Monument, Washington

Diablo Lake
North Cascades National Park, Washington

Good Morning
Okanagan (Places In Between), British Columbia, Canada

Catch of the Day
Kokanee Creek Provincial Park, British Columbia, Canada

Emerald Lake Reflections
Yoho National Park, British Columbia, Canada

Calm Before the Storm
Yoho National Park, British Columbia, Canada

Rogers Pass
Glacier National Park, British Columbia, Canada

Out for a Stroll
Jasper National Park, Alberta, Canada

Spirit Island
Jasper National Park, Alberta, Canada

Moraine Lake
Banff National Park, Alberta, Canada

Huckleberry Bear
Glacier National Park, Montana

Sunrise at Waterton
Waterton Lakes National Park, Alberta, Canada

Road to Many Glacier
Glacier National Park, Montana

Virginia Falls
Glacier
National Park,
Montana

Solitary Bison
Yellowstone National Park, Wyoming

Snowshoe Hare
Yellowstone National Park, Wyoming

Grand Canyon of the Yellowstone
Yellowstone National Park, Wyoming

Morning Glory Pool
Yellowstone National Park, Wyoming

Tetons Over Jackson Lake
Grand Teton National Park, Wyoming

Oxbow Bend Reflections
Grand Teton National Park, Wyoming

A Reason to Meet
Grand Teton National Park, Wyoming

Moulton Barn
Grand Teton National Park, Wyoming

Walking in the Rain
Grand Teton National Park, Wyoming

Giving Space
Laurance S. Rockefeller Preserve - Grand Teton National Park, Wyoming

Tower Storm
Devils Tower National Monument, Wyoming

Devils Tower
Devils Tower National Monument, Wyoming

Early Morning
Mount Rushmore National Memorial, South Dakota

Texas
Mount Rushmore National Memorial, South Dakota

Badlands Storm
Theodore Roosevelt National Park, North Dakota

Wild Horses and Bison
Theodore Roosevelt National Park, North Dakota

Gorge Trail
Watkins Glen State Park, New York

Ancient Stairway
Watkins Glen State Park,
New York

Vermont Fall
Green Mountain National Forest, Vermont

Acadia Fog
Acadia National Park, Maine

Sleepy Hollow Cemetery
Sleepy Hollow (Places in Between), New York

Memorial Reflections
Vietnam Veterans
National Memorial,
District of Columbia

Cider Apples
Old Mystic (Places in Between), Connecticut

Luray Caverns
Shenandoah National Park, Virginia

Myrtle Beach Pier
Myrtle Beach State Park, South Carolina

A Walk Through the Swamp
Congaree National Park, South Carolina

Snowy Fog
Great Smoky Mountains National Park, Tennessee

Great Smoky Mountains
Great Smoky Mountains National Park, Tennessee

Photographs from this book are featured in the traveling museum exhibit, *Exploring America,* celebrating America's National Parks.
For exhibit details, go to *www.ExploringAmericaExhibit.com*

Photographs are available for purchase on *www.HaresPhotography.com*

Photographer David Hares II is available for lectures for groups and conferences.

For information, please contact *info@HaresPhotography.com*

For information about special discounts for bulk purchases of this book, please contact Rabbit Press Special Sales.

Rabbit Press
P. O. Box 471624
Fort Worth, Texas 76147
Email: *RabbitPressPublishing@gmail.com*
Website: *RabbitPress.org*

Rabbit Press